LON CHANEY
— IN HIS OWN WORDS —

Compiled
by
Kevin Scott Collier

LON CHANEY
IN HIS OWN WORDS

LON CHANEY: IN HIS OWN WORDS, copyright 2017 Kevin Scott Collier. Sources: Photo-Play Journal, November 1917 / The Moving Picture Weekly, December 18, 1920 / Paramount and Metro Press Sheets, April-September 1923 / New York Radio transcript, 1923 / Picture-Play Magazine, May 1923 / American Cinematographer Magazine, 1925 / Photoplay Magazine, February 1928 / Picture-Play Magazine, March 1929 / New Movie Magazine, December 1929 / Picture Play, September 1930 / Internet Movie Database / Library of Congress newspapers 1912-1924 / Reference books and more. Visit the book page at: www.lonchaneytalks.blogspot.com. Email the author at: kevinscottcollier@yahoo.com.

THE FIRST WORDS

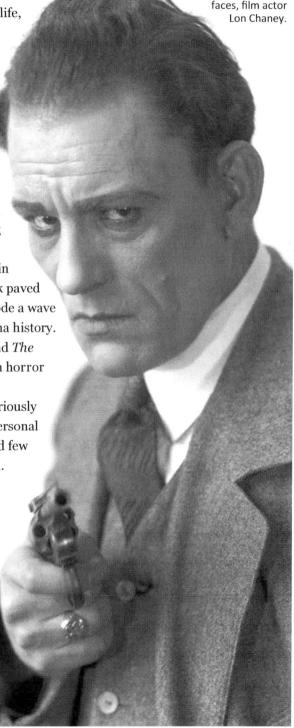

The man of a thousand faces, film actor Lon Chaney.

Lon Chaney didn't grant many interviews during his lifetime. He didn't like anyone snooping around in his personal life, and wished to be known for his work as an actor.

Myrtle Gebhart, a writer for Picture-Play magazine, spoke with Mr. Chaney and later wrote a piece on conducting interviews, in which she singled out 'the man of a thousand faces.'

"My hardest victim to corner was Lon Chaney," Gebhart wrote. "He frankly—and it isn't a pose—abhors publicity, because he wants people to remember the character he is portraying, not Lon Chaney. I wore out one set of tires and one disposition, mine, before I finally cornered him, and, bit by bit, dug his story out of him. I earned *that* check all right!"

Born on April Fool's Day, 1883, Chaney began acting in films in the year 1912. His innovative and creative work paved the way for the Universal Studios film monsters that rode a wave of popularity in the 1930's, and earned a place in cinema history.

His classic roles in *The Hunchback of Notre Dame* and *The Phantom of the Opera* are heralded as masterpieces in horror cinema.

The man who made his career in silent film was notoriously silent, away from the screen, regarding his work and personal life. Lon Chaney strongly disliked the press and allowed few interviews. He preferred that his work to speak for him.

During the filming of the film *Thunder*, Lon Chaney developed pneumonia. In late 1929, he was diagnosed with bronchial lung cancer. He died of a throat hemorrhage on August 26, 1930. His final interview hit the newsstands days later, in the September 1930 issue of *Picture Play* magazine.

Lon Chaney was 47 years old.

He leaves behind an incredible body of cinematic work, and a glimpse into his life and career, with the words left behind in the dusty pages of old magazines.

- Kevin Scott Collier

"My whole career has been devoted to keeping people from knowing me."
Lon Chaney

LON CHANEY IN HIS OWN WORDS

PERSONAL LIFE

"My home is my own. The public, I am sure, has no curiosity about my domestic life."

"I never go in for publicity. My life has not been extraordinary. It's been a hard life. There's nothing pretty to tell. I've fought—fought—fought—for everything that is mine. Nobody has ever given me a thing, with the exception of the public's approval that is coming to me now.

I've starved. I've labored. I've hungered for companionship, for the glad hand that speeds so many young fellows on their way.

I've often wondered, when things were so black, why I've kept on, if I shouldn't give up and drift as I saw others doing. But there was something in me that wouldn't let me stop.

Not ambition.

I have no personal ambition, no craving for fame. That's why I don't care for publicity—I'd rather the public would know nothing about Lon Chaney. For only in his complete submergence am I able to make my characterizations convincing."

"My parents were deaf-mutes. Perfectly normal in every other way. Splendid minds. So, as a child, I learned to express my every wish on my face. I could talk on my fingers, the sign language of the deaf-mutes, before I could speak.

But as I grew older I found it unnecessary. We conversed with our faces, with our eyes.

My grandmother founded the first Deaf and Blind Institute in Colorado, and my mother was stage director there. So I early developed a longing to go on the stage and did so at the age of ten, after a few years in the public schools of Colorado Springs. At eighteen I was a stagehand at twelve dollars a week. Later, I was combination stagehand, chorus man, and wardrobe mistress—yes, mistress—at the stupendous weekly salary of fourteen dollars.

We children possessed all of our faculties, but it devolved upon me to raise my brother and sister and to care for my parents."

"My parents were deaf mutes, but we belonged to the white-collar class. I only got through the fourth grade, but don't a lot of kids in normal homes go to work early, to help out? I was a prop

boy in a theater at Colorado Springs.

I watched the actors, copied the performers, until I could sing and dance. I first appeared at sixteen, in a stagehand benefit. I still carry my membership card.

I feel sorry for the fellow who gets licked, if he really has tried. For the one handicapped, either physically or mentally. For those who take their medicine of punishment manfully. For those who have made mistakes and are feeling their way to the light, to the right."

"Tonight I start out for the high Sierras. No shaving, no make-up, no interviewers for four long, lazy weeks. We take a stove along and the wife cooks the fish I catch. We sleep under the pines and I try to climb high enough to reach the snows. Camping's the biggest kick in life for me."

"I've been cooking, that's my hobby, really. I'm proud of my Italian and French dishes. You see, my wife is Italian and I am of French descent, so we are pretty good culinary partners."

"When I go on a holiday [vacation], I forget work completely."

EARLY CAREER

"I played in comic opera when I wanted to do tragic drama. I felt tragic, somber. I didn't laugh and play like other children. I was born with a sense of responsibility. I couldn't waste time. So I danced—but not for joy. Because it was the only way they would let me earn a living. I didn't want to dance.

I was one of those pink-tinted chorus men in 'The Time, the Place, and the Girl,' 'The Royal Chef,' and 'A Knight for a Day.'

Then I played in 'The Mikado' and was the valet in 'The Little Tycoon.' An eccentric dancer, almost a clown, in cheap musical comedies."

"I alternated between comedies and one-reel Westerns at Universal. We slapped pictures together in two days to a week. I must have been in at least a hundred. Only a few names stick. I remember a joker comedy called, 'Back to Life,' another titled 'Red Margaret.' I was a moonshiner hidden among the rocks in that one.

The chief thing for me was that I got three dollar checks daily and that occasionally they were worth that. The movies had their forces at work but none of us quite sensed the gigantic thing we were mixed up with.

Some of the troupe were getting somewhere, but I wasn't in that class. The big stars on our lot were J. Warren Kerrigan and Jeanie Macpherson.

First, she [Macpherson] was a lady. Then she had a foreign education, had played Broadway, had worked under D. W. Griffith in New York, and finally she had the ability to write as well as act in her own pictures. She wrote and acted in a feature a week. I've forgotten the name of the one

in which she first cast me, but I do remember that if she had been anyone else I would have refused to play the scene. It was straight character drama and I was convinced I was a comedian.

I had to be an outraged husband who discovered his wife in another man's arms. Desperately, I walked into the scene and started calling my wife names. I had done a lot of listening in my life and I discovered I had quite a store of names to call an erring wife. I raved on until Miss Macpherson's laughter stopped me. I thought that finished me, but she was only laughing at my vehemence. She then directed me through the scene, ordering me to keep my mouth shut."

"We [our stage company in my early years as a performer] toured from Canada to Florida, but the closest we came to New York was Buffalo. We played all the flag stations. At one place down in Oklahoma, the owner of the opera house was questioned by the manager as to whether he had 'hard' tickets. 'Oh, yes!' said the rural Belasco. I got two color of tickets. Later in the evening he rushed to our ticket taker and said, 'I well-nigh forgot to tell you that the yellow tickets are pints, them's for children. The green tickets are quarts, them's for adults.'"

"The curly-haired boys and girls were then holding forth. Character work meant nothing. I went from one studio to the other but I soon discovered I was totally unknown except at Universal. At first I wasn't frightened. I had saved my money in those six years. I had a little home and my boy was going to school. But as the weeks became months I began to believe [William] Sistrom wasn't such an idiot. Then Bill Hart saved my life."

CAREER & THE INDUSTRY

"My whole career has been devoted to keeping people from knowing me."

"Nine years ago, I went into pictures. Played the heavy in 'Hell Morgan's Girl.' I had no one to teach me make-up. I had to teach myself, by observing characters on the street and attempting to copy them.

I've spent hours striving to make my face over to resemble some convict's I had seen in the city jail or some slant-eyed Chinaman whom I had surreptitiously studied down in the mystic byways of Chinatown.

When I gained an effect, with the aid of a few false hairs and adhesive tape, I felt as I imagine

an author feels when he completes a good book or an artist when he finishes a painting that has long baffled him.

I stayed with Universal for five years. Four years ago I started to freelance, determined to get the parts I wanted, or starve. My wife stood behind me. It wasn't easy—and there were the kiddies to consider. I could have signed up, but not to do the roles I wanted. So we stuck it out, the wife and I."

"Even among all those other terrible actors I couldn't be important. The only person who was aware of my existence was myself."

"As for the real Lon Chaney, it's in my pictures. I've tried to show that the lowliest people frequently have the highest ideals. In the lower depths, when life hasn't been too pleasant for me, I've always had that gentleness of feeling, that compassion of an underdog for a fellow sufferer. 'The Hunchback' was an example of it. So was 'The Unknown' and, in a different class of society, 'Mr. Wu.'"

"I try to bring that emotion to the screen. Beyond that I don't fuss. People seem to have the impression I study scripts all the time. I don't. I don't even try to find stories for myself like some stars. I wouldn't know where to look for them and I probably would not recognize them if I found them.

I trust my producers to look out for my good. All I want to know is what the character is like and what emotions rule him. It takes me two to four weeks to work out a make-up for a new picture. That set, I don't worry.

I've had good directors. Tod Browning and I have worked so much together he's called the Chaney director. I like his work. I think Victor Seastrom and Benjamin Christonson are great directors. Their values are finer. But I really don't worry over who they hand me.

The chief thing for any actor to remember is that it wasn't his brains that got him to stardom. It was only his acting. He isn't paid to think about production plans, and when he starts to, he usually sinks his whole career."

"I don't consider fan mail representative of public opinion. Only certain classes, types, and ages write an actor, as a rule. Many of the older, mature people don't, yet they are regular patrons. The box office is the only real guide; it is the public's spokesman. I follow exhibitors' reports in the trade magazines."

"I've said my say about them [talking motion pictures] pretty often, but perhaps they misunderstood my meaning. They seem to take it for granted I won't talk, at all. I didn't ever say that, but I want to wait a while. I didn't think the thing was perfected so that a man could get a real human quality into it. They say that they've done wonderful things lately. I want to see when I get back. I'm not afraid of the talker. Dean Immell, of the University of Southern California, is an expert, and he listened in on my 'squeaking.' He says my voice is okay. I was on the stage before I ever thought of pictures, and my voice seemed to get across there without any trouble. Taking these lumps [surgically] out of my throat ought to help it. [It's] sort of difficult to talk across a couple of baking-size potatoes."

"Disillusionment was inevitable, once the screen got sound. The talkies are making pictures more realistic, shattering that optical vacuity, that romantic make-believe which camera magic has made possible to a degree, far beyond the stage's possibilities.

In some respects, I welcome sound. It adds depth and actuality to situations and to individual performance. For myself. I regret it. My odd characters, though founded on life, have been made imaginative for emphasis.

That realism which in the human voice will dispel the mystery instantly, I am afraid. Now, I must use less physical make-up, if allowance is to be made for vocal effects. It will mean a shifting of the burden, a sharing of it, in creating a characterization. I must express vocally some of the traits and idiosyncrasies of the person. But there isn't a lot one can do with the voice."

THE ART OF ACTING

"Acting is mainly a matter of thinking. If you think the part you are playing, invariably you will portray it—accurately and with power. I've fre-

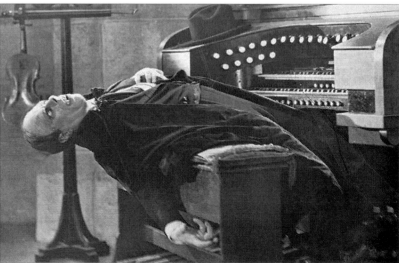

quently told young actors who have come to me for advice, 'Do your acting in your head and forget about your body.' If you think the man you are playing, you'll be that man."

"The parts I play point out a moral. They show individuals who might have been different, if they had been given a different chance."

"I've never read but two scripts previous to the start of production. If the company gives me bad pictures, it costs them money."

"Acting is feeling expressed through technique. I must feel a character's reactions thoroughly. But the expression of that emotion cannot be left to impulse. Think it [over], figure out in what form such a person would show each feeling. I sit for hours, making mental faces.

The trouble with youth [actors] is, they won't concentrate. They dog the studios for work, and when they can't get it, they fritter their time away whining about tough luck, or dreaming of what they'll do when they're famous. Instead, after making the rounds of the studios, a young fellow should go home and think, visualizing different types of people, meditating, 'Suppose I were such-and-such, how would I feel and act?'

Success is a hit-and-miss proposition, but if crude talent is there, it will shine through poor roles eventually."

"To be wicked is to my mind one of the most difficult things for an actor to undertake. And at the same time, it is one of the most infinitely interesting and fascinating sides of the actor's art."

"Nobody is ever sorry for a man who is sorry for himself. If I'm playing a pathetic part on the screen, I never get to feeling it so hard that I'm sorry for myself, even in character. I always tell the director, 'If I start looking as though I'm feeling sorry for myself, stop me.' That's no way to get sympathy from people, even in pictures."

"One of the most difficult characters I ever played from the make-up standpoint was that of a blind boy. All through that picture, in order to look blind, I had to roll my eyes clear up in what seemed to me to be the very top of my head. Did you ever try to do that? Try it, and then at the same time try to act naturally. You'll get my idea then."

"Most of my roles since 'The Hunchback of Notre Dame' (1923), such as 'The Phantom of the Opera' (1925), 'He Who Gets Slapped' (1924), 'The

'Unholy Three (1925), etc., have carried the theme of self-sacrifice or renunciation. These are the stories which I wish to do."

"Motion picture acting is pantomime highly developed and aided by the use of a few subtitles. I feel that the circumstances under which I lived as a boy helped me a great deal in pantomime acting. If you will take time to notice the next time you see two or more deaf mutes in conversation, you will see that they resort to the use of the finger sign language but little, comparatively speaking. One glance conveys a whole paragraph. Just try to carry on a wordless conversation with someone and you will soon learn that it takes endless patience to perfect gestures and facial expressions—and the worst fault of all, to my way of thinking, is over acting or exaggeration of gesture."

THE MIRACLE MAN (1919)

"'The Miracle Man' is the only perfect film [I was in] ever produced."

"George Tucker didn't really want me for the role of the cripple in 'The Miracle Man.' He wanted a professional contortionist, but the five he had already tried out in the part couldn't act it. When Tucker described the part to me I knew my whole future rested on me getting it.

Tucker explained that the first scene he would shoot would be the one where the fake cripple unwound himself before his pals. If I could do that, I got the job.

I went home to try to think it out. I'm not a contortionist, of course. It would have been easier lots of times in my subsequent work if I had been. While I was sitting, pondering over that part I unconsciously did a trick we have done since childhood. I crossed my legs, then double crossed them, wrapping my left foot around my right ankle.

I caught sight of myself in the mirror and jumped up to try walking that way. I found I could do it with a little practice. Then I rushed out to buy the right clothes.

When I came to the studio on the test day, Tucker was already behind the camera. He gave me one glance and called 'Camera.' I flopped down, dragging myself forward along the floor, my eyes rolling, my face twitching and my legs wrapping tighter and tighter around each other. Tucker didn't speak and the sweat rolled off me. Finally I heard a single whispered word from him. 'God,' Tucker said. I wanted to say that too, but not for the same reason."

"George Loane Tucker called me for the part of The Frog [in 'The Miracle Worker'] without explaining it or the nature of the picture. He simply asked if I could play a cripple. 'Certainly,' was my answer.

Mr. Tucker was not convinced because he knew the miraculous transformation that had to be performed. He wouldn't tell me of this. The story was being kept a secret from everyone. He asked me to give a demonstration of what I could do. That seemed unreasonable to me.

Mr. Tucker was familiar with my work and knew the range of characters I have played. So, I refused. Finally, after considerable debate, he assigned me the part. I went to the studio with a mental outline of my make-up. I would wear a wooden leg, place a hump on one shoulder, and roll my eyes back as though blind.

Oh, I was quite sure of myself.

Then Mr. Tucker took me aside and told me the story. 'You are to enter a groveling, deformed paralytic, then you are to arise up before the camera a cured, whole man,' said he. I was beaten. That's all; I was beaten. But I was determined not to show my defeat.

I said, 'I can do it.' Mr. Tucker was still skeptical. The day came when I was to do the big scene of the picture. It was the first scene taken—that of the fake cure. I knew I could twist my hands and roll my eyes back into my head—but that's all I did know.

'Lights! Camera!' called Mr. Tucker. 'All right, Mr. Chaney.' Up until that moment, I didn't know what I should do. I just had faith that I could do it some way. Then, like a flash, I remembered a dance I did years ago in musical shows. It ended with a sort of whirl and twist of the legs. I threw myself on the floor, twisted my legs and hands, rolled my eyes back into my head, a fluid make-up streaming like matter from the eyes, and I squirmed over the floor toward the camera.

'Ugh!' exclaimed Mr. Tucker. 'That's horrible. We can never show the public a close-up of that face!' And they never have. It really was a miracle to me—that sudden conception of how I might appear a twisted, limp, repulsive rag of a man, and then suddenly transfigure—directly before the camera—into one physically sound."

"Tucker would have preferred a contortionist, but none of them could act the role. So I practiced, studying, imitating until I got it.

Then came Blizzard in 'The Penalty.' I strapped my legs back. The pain was intense; we had to stop every few minutes so that I could remove the straps and massage my legs, which grew numb.

But no more cripple parts. I'm too stove-up from my years of dancing.

Though I have played practically every nationality, I prefer Orientals.

The Latin races are too expressive, they talk with their hands, with gestures; but portraying the Celestial is infinite art.

He is passive, repressed; by thought alone, I have put over my three Chinese roles.

I get my types on the street, spend my evenings in the foreign sections of Los Angeles, studying the immigrants, acquainting myself not alone with their facial and racial characteristics but their inner complexes."

THE HUNCHBACK OF NOTRE DAME (1923)

"The idea of doing the picture was an old one of mine, and I had studied Quasimodo until I knew him like a brother. I knew every ghoulish impulse of his heart and all the inarticulate miseries of his soul.

Quasimodo and I lived together—until we became one. At least so it has since seemed to me. When I played him, I forgot my own identity completely and for the time being lived and suffered with 'The Hunchback of Notre Dame.'"

"I wanted to remind people that the lowest types of humanity may have within them the capacity for supreme self-sacrifice. The dwarfed, misshapen beggar of the streets may have the noblest ideals. Most of my roles have carried the theme of self-sacrifice or renunciation. These are the stories I wish to do."

"I have made two personal appearances [in motion pictures as favors]. Once, with 'The Hunchback of Notre Dame,' because I didn't know any better.

The second time, with 'Tell It to the Marines,' as a courtesy to General Butler and the government for cooperation given us while making the picture. But never again."

LAUGH, CLOWN, LAUGH (1924)

"There's nothing funny about a clown in the moonlight."

PHANTOM OF THE OPERA (1925)

[To the cinematographer Virgil Miller] "I said, Virg, make me look frightening and repulsive, but at the same time, make the audience love me."

MASTER OF DISGUISE

"When a makeup is as painful as that which I wore as Blizzard in 'The Penalty' (1920), when I had my legs strapped up and couldn't bear it that way more than 20 minutes at a time—when I have to be a cripple, as in 'The Miracle Man' (1919) or have to keep a certain attitude of body, as I did in 'Shadows' (1922), it sometimes takes a good deal of imagination to forget your physical sufferings. Yet, at that, the subconscious mind has a marvelous way of making you keep the right attitudes and make the right gestures when you are actually acting."

"I hope I shall never be accused of striving merely for horrible effects."

"In 'Tell It to the Marines,' I never had a bit of make-up on during the entire shooting of that picture, and I played it straight."

"I wrote the piece [about make-up] for the Encyclopedia Britannica. Should an author show his own mug on what he has written? Do you print your own picture? Besides, it's my business to keep being a mystery. I didn't care about having them see Lon Chaney go through all his secrets. I admired their make-up [Emil Jannings and Conrad Veidt] and [including their photos] made good illustrations [to accompany the article]. I don't see any sense in hogging the whole show."

"One of the hardest make-ups I ever carried over was that of King Canute. He was hairy of face, and breast, and I had besides to use putty to build out my nose and cheeks. One day I tried wax instead and my nose—pardon me, Miss—began to run when the sun got hot!"

"How do I build my cheeks out to a semblance of fat and well-fed prosperity? My dear young woman, I do not scorn for this purpose the humble chewing gum. I tuck this away inside my cheeks, next to my gums. But there's a knack about doing it right, I'll admit. And those plump hands which you behold grow on me when I'm a fat and prosperous plutocrat? Rubber gloves. They are specially made, and they are worn over a well-fitting pair of kid gloves, so as not to wrinkle. You see my hands are rather small, which makes the added size possible."

"As for my hair, 'I'm glad it's all there,' as the poet says; yet in character parts, life is just one wig after another. I have had mine all made especially, and I keep them labelled and carefully put away, having them examined once a month for moths. I have a collection of more than one hundred of these wigs and you'd be surprised to know the investment they represent.

You know one of the most effective disguises is the hair and the way in which it is combed. I always make my own serve whenever I can, and to make silvery hair, I use neck white—if you know what that is.

Some people use aluminum, but that shows too much on the screen. I used it once and my hair and it caused halation in the picture. I was supposed to be a hoary old scoundrel, although it made me look like a halo trimmed saint."

"Of course, make-up goes much deeper than mere wrinkles or whispers of greasepaint. No, I

don't mean thought, this time—though of course that's the principal part. I mean you must study all the previous history of the character and realize its effect on his physical being.

For instance. in playing a music-master, once, who, constantly led an orchestra with his bow or baton, I made him all through the picture appear just a bit higher in the right shoulder than in the left. Men in different walk of life have little subtle differences in the manner in which they carry themselves. Some of these are psychological effects, and others come from the nature of their occupations."

"The hardest character I ever played from the make-up standpoint? I think it was that of a blind boy. All through, in order to make my eyes have that terrible, sightless look, I rolled them clear up in my head. Did you ever try to do that? And then did you ever try to hold them in that position, and not only hold them so, but go on acting in a natural manner? There were many trying scenes in the picture, and I suffered from that abnormal eye position for days afterward."

ADVICE TO BORIS KARLOFF

"Find something no one else can or will do. The secret of success in movies lies in being different from anyone else."

LON CHANEY JR.

"He [my son Lon Chaney Jr.] is six-feet-two. That's too tall [to be an actor]. He would always have had to have parts built around him. He couldn't build himself for the part. Besides, he's happy in business, and he's got a great wife. They are grand kids."

More on page 40

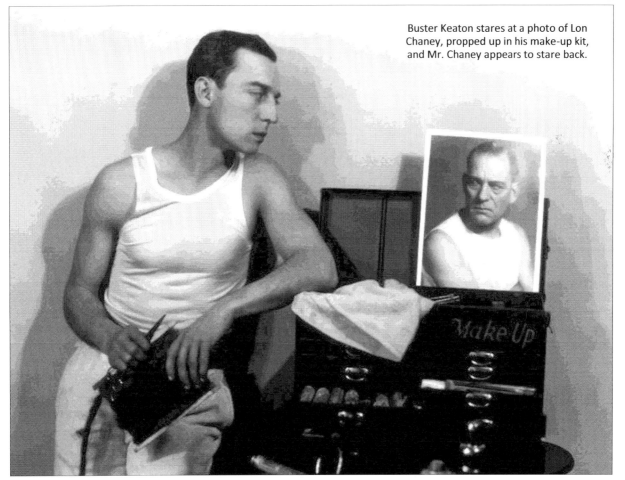

Buster Keaton stares at a photo of Lon Chaney, propped up in his make-up kit, and Mr. Chaney appears to stare back.

"The Miracle Man"
(1919)

"Treasure Island" (1920)

"Treasure Island" (1920)

"Bits of Life"
(1921)

"A Blind Bargain"
(1922)

"The Hunchback of Notre Dame" (1923)

"The Hunchback of Notre Dame" (1923)

"The Hunchback of Notre Dame" (1923)

"He Who Gets Slapped" (1924)

"He Who Gets Slapped"
(1924)

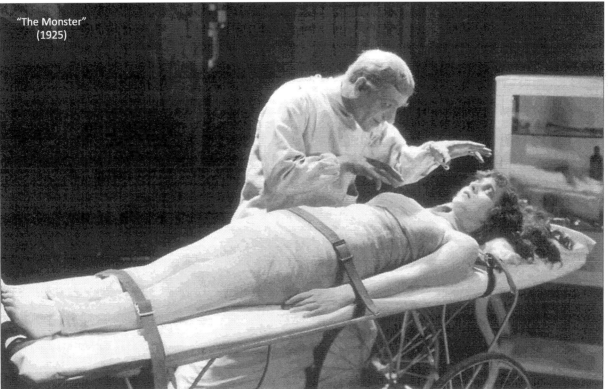
"The Monster"
(1925)

"The Monster"
(1925)

"The Phantom of the Opera" (1925)

"The Phantom of the Opera" (1925)

"The Phantom of the Opera" (1925)

"The Tower of Lies" (1925)

"The Unholy Three"
(1925)

"The Road to Mandalay" (1926)

"Tell it to the Marines" (1926)

"Mr. Wu" (1927)

"London After Midnight" (1927)

"London After Midnight" (1927)

"West of Zanzibar"
(1928)

"Laugh, Clown, Laugh" (1928)

"While the City Sleeps" (1928)

"The Unholy Three" (1930)

"The Unholy Three"
(1930)

THE FINAL WORD

DISTASTE FOR INTERVIEWS

"Bickford's line is, 'Quit, but don't let 'em let you.' Mine is, 'Don't give 'em an interview, but don't let 'em get away without it.'

Well, I mean it.

I should never have opened my mouth. My judgment was correct. It proved to be bad business. It dispelled the mystery attached to my type of characters. I was misquoted. The reaction was noticeable in fan mail, and among my friends, few of whom are professionals.

All expressed surprise when they read the things I was supposed to have said. Remarks attributed to me did not conform to my screen work, nor did they seem consistent to those who know me. I stopped talking, except in non-committal fashion.

I said 'Yes,' 'No,' and 'Uh-huh,' and let it go at that. But reporters are ingenious. They managed to distort even my monosyllabic comments.

Women are more fertile in imagination, but the men reporters are as big [of] liars, though with less finesse. Women have a gift for making the unreal seem true, by weaving into their stories an artistic detail, whereas men, if more blunt, are just as willing to misquote in order to make a sensational story."

"I've answered more questions than I ever dreamed could be asked. Nobody but my wife and the boy, and his wife, and our chauffeur knows where that camp is. And nobody else will ever find out. They've gone up there ahead of me. But I'm starting right out there this moment. Good-bye, and good luck to you."

"Well, if you know so much [about my contract with M. G. M.], why do you ask me about it? Say, young lady; you asked enough questions."

"Say, I told you once before that if I had my way I'd never have an interview. I want to be a mystery. Don't you remember?"

"The story's over. Have you gotten a philosophy of life out of it all?"

ILLNESS LAST YEAR OF LIFE

"I'll be out of this place [the hospital] in a week, and the doc says that after a rest to get back my weight, I'll be a new man. And believe me, they've got a strenuous program laid out then, for I have to catch up for the time I've lost [from] being sick.

You know, under my contract, if I'm sick, I have to make up the time and deliver productions by intensive work.

What are they [the press] trying to do to me? First they report me laid up, even say I have T. B., and now they rumor me out of pictures! I can't even be sick.

Me leaving the screen [retiring] is just about as silly as that rumor about my having tuberculosis, which I haven't. T. B. bugs like young and tender meat. I'm too old and tough for them to pay me any attention.

I wish you'd tell them for me that any guy's got a right to be sick once in his life, and I'd appreciate it if they'd let me do it in comfort. Not that comfort's the right word for this kind of thing.

Do you know they had to fatten me [up] just like a pig getting ready to be butchered?

They sent me off to the Hot Springs to eat and lie in the sun so I could get ready for the butcher. But I put one over on them. I sneaked across the border for some hunting. Put one over on them here, too. Nobody knew I was coming. Had them

out and didn't tell a person.

I don't remember the first night. Good thing, I guess. When a fellow gets to be in his forties, the knife is sort of unnatural to him. How did I get sick? I had pneumonia.

Went over to Wisconsin and played around in the snow for my last picture, 'Thunder,' they called it. 'Snow' would have been better. I wasn't used to it, or the cold, either!

Living in California sort of makes you forget that you come from Denver, Colorado.

[I got] Pneumonia. I guess that's sort of likely to be serious. People tried to tell me to stay in bed, but I'm not much of a sick person. The nurse will verify that statement.

I went back to finish the picture and then it sort of started all over again. Illness is all that prevented me being at the studio right now. I ought to be there.

The last picture I made is already being released, and I'll have to hustle like the dickens to keep them up to schedule.

I squawked my head off about this operation. I didn't want flowers and telephone calls and letters."

RETIREMENT & FUTURE

"I have attained a position where I don't have to double cross my convictions. I have signed a five-year contract on my own terms. On its completion, I will have reached my financial goal and will quit. I have worked hard all my life, the past eighteen years in pictures, and will be entitled, then, to retire."

"Nope [concerning returning to the stage after retiring from motion pictures]. I'll be through with acting. I want to travel. No particular countries, just the wanderlust, to look for odd characters. I'm interested more in places than in people, now. Human nature is the same the world over, with [only] slight variations."

"Would I write my memoirs? Not by a jugful. My personal life is nobody's business. Besides, I lack the patience to write. I can't get thoughts into words. I can sit for hours experimenting with make-up, or 'thinking' my work; but I can express my thoughts fluently only in terms of facial expression. And, I'll fix it so that nobody will write my biography after I'm gone, too."

CHANEY FILM LISTING

1912

"The Honor of the Family," released November 7, role unconfirmed.

1913

"The Ways of Fate." released April 19, role unknown / "Suspense," released July 6, cast in the role of a hobo / "Poor Jake's Demise," released August 16, cast in the role of the Dude / "The Sea Urchin," released August 22, cast in the role of Barnacle Bill / "The Blood Red Tape of Charity," released September 26, cast in the role of Marx, a gentleman thief / "Shon the Piper," released September 30, cast in the role of a Clansman / "The Trap," released October 3, cast in the role of Lon / "The Restless Spirit," released October 27, cast in the role of Tthe Russian Count / "Almost an Actress," released November 15, cast in the role of the cameraman / "An Elephant on His Hands," released November 21, cast in the role of Eddie's uncle / "Back to Life," released November 24, cast in the role of the rival / "Red Margaret, Moonshiner," released December 2, cast in the role of Lon / "Bloodhounds of the North," released December 23, cast in the role of a Mountie lieutenant.

1914

"The Lie," released January 6, cast in the role of young MacGregor / "The Honor of the Mounted," released February 17, cast in the role of Jacques Laquox / "Remember Mary Magdalen," released February 23, cast in the role of the half-wit / "Discord and Harmony," released March 17, cast in the role of Lon, the sculptor / "The Menace to Carlotta," released March 22, cast in the role of Giovanni Bartholdi / "The Embezzler," released March 31, cast in the role of J. Roger Dixon / "The Lamb, the Woman, the Wolf," released April 4, cast in the role of the wolf / "The End of the Feud," released April 12, cast in the role of Wood Dawson / "The Tragedy of Whispering Creek," released May 2, cast in the role of the greaser / "The Unlawful Trade," released May 14, cast in the role of the cross-blood / "Heart Strings," released June 5, role is unconfirmed / "The Forbidden Room," released June 20, cast in the role of John Morris / "The Old Cobbler," released June 27, cast in the role of Wild Bill / "The Hopes of Blind Alley," released July 4, cast in the role of the vendor / "A Ranch Romance," released July 8, cast in the role of Raphael Praz / "Her Grave Mistake," released July 15, cast in the role of Nunez / "By the Sun's Rays," released July 22, cast in the role of Frank Lawler, the clerk / "The Trey o' Hearts," released August 4, cast in the role of one of Judith's henchmen / "The Oubliette," released August 15, cast in the role of Chevalier Bertrand de la Payne / "A Miner's Romance," released August 26, cast in the role of John Burns / "Her Bounty," released September

13, cast in the role of Fred Howard / "The Higher Law," released September 19, cast in the role of Sir Stephen Fitz Allen / Richelieu," released September 26, cast in the role of Baradas / "The Pipes O' Pan," released October 4, cast in the role of Arthur Darrell / "Virtue Is Its Own Reward," released October 11, cast in the role of Duncan Bronson / "Her Life's Story," released October 15, cast in the role of Don Valesquez / "Damon and Pythias." released November 23, cast in the role of the wild man / "Light and Shadows." released November 29, cast in the role of Bentley / "The Lion, the Lamb, the Man," released December 6, cast in the role of Fred Brown, and the lion / "A Night of Thrills," released December 13, cast in the role of the visitor / "Her Escape," released December 27, cast in the role of Pete Walsh, Pauline's brother.

1915 *

"The Sin of Olga Brandt," released January 3, cast in the role of Stephen Leslie / "The Star of the Sea," released January 10, cast in the role of Tomasco, a fisherman / "A Small Town Girl," released January 17, cast in the role of the procurer / "The Measure of a Man," released January 28, cast in the role of Donald MacDermott / "The Threads of Fate," released February 21, cast in the role of the Count / "When the Gods Played a Badger Game," released February 28, cast in the role of Joe, the property man / "Such Is Life," released March 4, cast in the role of Tod Wilkes / "Where the Forest Ends," released March 7, cast in the role of Paul Rouchelle / "Outside the Gates," released March 14, cast in the role of Perez / "All for Peggy," released March 18, cast in the role of Seth Baldwin / "The Desert Breed," released March 28, cast in the role of Fred / "Maid of the Mist," released April 1, cast in the role of Lin, Pauline's father / "The Grind," released April 11, cast in the role of Henry Leslie / "The Girl of the Night," released April 18, cast in the role of Jerry / "The Stool Pigeon," released April 19, cast in an unknown role / "An Idyll of the Hills," released May 13, cast in the role of Lafe Jameson / "The Stronger Mind," released May 15, cast in the role of the crook's pal / "The Oyster Dredger," released June 14, cast in an unknown role / "Steady Company," released July 6, cast in the role of Jimmy Ford / "The Violin Maker," released July 9, cast in the role of Pedro the violin maker / "The Trust," released July 16, cast in the role of Jim Mason / "Bound on the Wheel," released July 25, cast in the role of Tom Coulahan / "Mountain Justice," released August 15, cast in the role of Jeffrey Kirke / "Quits," released August 17, cast in the role of Frenchy / "The Chimney's Secret," released August 16, cast in the role of Charles Harding / "The Pine's Revenge," released September 19, cast in the role of Black

Scotty / "The Fascination of the Fleur de Lis," released September 26, cast in the role of the Duke of Safoulrug / "Alas and Alack," released October 10, cast in the roles of the fisherman and Hunchback Fate / "A Mother's Atonement," released October 17, cast in the role of Ben Morrison / "Lon of Lone Mountain," released October 19, cast in the role of Lon Moore / "The Millionaire Paupers," released October 26, cast in the role of Martin, the landlord / "Under a Shadow," released December 5, cast in the role of DeSerris / "Father and the Boys," released December 20, cast in the role of Mr. Tuck Bartholomew / "Stronger Than Death," released December 26, cast in the role of the attorney.

1916

"Dolly's Scoop," released February 20, cast in the role of Dan Fisher / "The Grip of Jealousy," released February 28, cast in the role of Silas Lacey / "Tangled Hearts," released April 2, cast in the role of John Hammond / "The Gilded Spider," released May 8, cast in the role of Giovanni / "Bobbie of the Ballet," released June 12, cast in the role of Hook Hoover / "The Grasp of Greed," released June 17, cast in the role of Jimmie / "The Mark of Cain," released August 7, cast in the role of Dick Temple / "If My Country Should Call," released September 26. cast in the role of Dr. George Ardrath / "Felix on the Job," released October 31, cast in the role of Tad / "The Place Beyond the Winds," released November 6, cast in the role of Jerry Jo / "Accusing Evidence," released November 23, role unknown / "The Price of Silence," released December 11, cast in the role of Edmond Stafford.

1917

"The Piper's Price," released January 8, cast in the role of Billy Kilmartin / "Hell Morgan's Girl,"

released March 5, cast in the role of Sleter Noble / "The Mask of Love," released March 29, cast in the role of Marino / "The Girl in the Checkered Coat," released April 23, cast in the role of Hector Maitland / "The Flashlight," released May 21, cast in the roles of Henry Norton and Porter Brixton / "A Doll's House," released June 11, cast in the role of Nils Krogstad / "Fires of the Rebellion," released July 2, cast in the role of Russell Hanlon / "The Rescue," released July 30, cast in the role of Thomas Holland / "Pay Me!" released September 1, cast in the role of Joe Lawson / "Triumph," released September 3, cast in the role of Paul Neihoff / "The Empty Gun," released September 4, cast in the role of Frank / "Anything Once," released October 8, cast in the role of Waughnt Moore / "Bondage," released October 17, cast in the role of the seducer / "The Scarlet Car," released December 24, cast in the role of Paul Revere Forbes.

1918

"Broadway Love," released January 21, cast in the role of Elmer Watkins / "The Grand Passion," released February 1, cast in the role of Paul Argos / "The Kaiser, the Beast of Berlin," released March 9, cast in the role of Bethmann Hollweg / "Fast Company," released April 1, cast in the role of Dan McCarty / "A Broadway Scandal," released June 1, cast in the role of Kink Colby / "Riddle Gawne," released August 3, cast in the role of Hame Bozzam / "That Devil, Bateese," released September 2, cast in the role of Louis Courteau / "The Talk of the Town," released September 28, cast in the role of Jack Langhorne / "Danger, Go Slow," released December 16, cast in the role of Bud.

1919

"The Wicked Darling," released February 24, cast in the role of Stoop Connors / "The False Faces," released February 16, cast in the role of Karl Eckstrom / "A Man's Country," released July 13, cast in the role of Three Card Duncan / "The Miracle Man," released August 26, cast in the role of the Frog / "Paid in Advance," released November 30, cast in the role of Bateese Le Blanc / "When Bearcat Went Dry," released November 2, cast in the role of Kindard Powers / "Victory," released December 7, cast in the role of Ricardo.

1920

"Daredevil Jack," released February 15, cast in the role of Royce Rivers / "Treasure Island," released April 4, cast in the roles of Blind Pew and Merry / "The Gift Supreme," released April, cast in the role of Merney Stagg / "The Penalty," released June 3, cast in the role of Blizzard / "Nomads of the North," released September 26, cast in the role of Raoul Challoner.

1921

"Outside the Law," released January 6, cast in the roles of Black Mike Sylva and Ah Wing / "The Ace of Hearts," released April 24, cast in the role

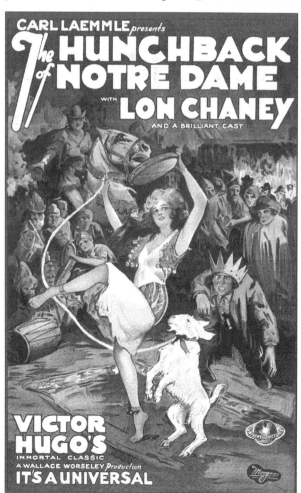

of Farallone / "For Those We Love," released September, cast in the role of Trix Ulner / "Bit of Life," released September 26, cast in the role of Chin Chow / "Voices of the City," released December, cast in the role of O'Rourke.

1922

"The Trap," released May 9, cast in the role of Gaspard the Good / "Flesh and Blood," released August 27, cast in the role of David Webster / "The Light in the Dark," released September 3, cast in the role of Tony Pantelli / "Oliver Twist," released October 30, cast in the role of Fagin / "Shadows," released November 10, cast in the roles of Yen Sin and the heathen / "Quincy Adams Sawyer," released December 4, cast in the role of Obadiah Strout / "A Blind Bargain," released December 3, cast in the roles of Dr. Arthur Lamb and the ape man.

1923

"All the Brothers Were Valiant," released January 15, cast in the role of Mark Shore / "While Paris Sleeps," released January 21, cast in the role of Henri Santodos / "The Shock," released June 10, cast in the role of Wilse Dilling / "The Hunchback of Notre Dame," released September 6, cast in the role of Quasimodo.

1924

"The Next Corner," released February 18, cast in the role of Juan Serafin / "He Who Gets Slapped," released December 22, cast in the role of Paul Beaumont.

1925

"The Monster," released March 16, cast in the role of Dr. Ziska / "The Unholy Three," released August 16, cast in the role of Echo, the ventrilo-

quist / "Tower of Lies," released October 11, cast in the role of Jan / "Phantom of the Opera," released November 15, Cast in the role of the Phantom.

1926

"The Blackbird," released February 13, cast in the roles of Dan, the Blackbird and the Bishop / "The Road to Mandalay," released June 28, cast in the role of Singapore Joe.

1927

"Tell It to the Marines," released January 29, cast in the role of Sergeant O'Hara / "Mr. Wu," released March 26, cast in the roles of Mr. Wu and Wu's grandfather / "The Unknown," released June 4, cast in the role of Alonzo / "Mockery," released August 13, cast in the role of Sergei / "London After Midnight," released December 3, cast in the role of Professor Edward C. Burke.

1928

"The Big City," released March 24, cast in the role of Chuck Collins / "Laugh, Clown, Laugh," released April 14, cast in the role of Tito / "While the City Sleeps," released September 15, cast in the role of Dan Coghlan / "West of Zanzibar," released August 13, cast in the role of Phroso.

1929

"Where East is East," released May 4, cast in the role of Tiger Haynes / "Thunder," released July 8, cast in the role of Grumpy Anderson.

1930

"The Unholy Three," remake of 1925 film, released July 12, cast in the role of Echo. Lon Chaney's only sound motion picture.

What did he hide behind his painted smile

Made in the USA
Lexington, KY
26 June 2019